BRIGHTON & H[

THEN AND NOW – VOLUME II

CHRISTOPHER HORLOCK

S.B. Publications

DEDICATION

This book is dedicated to the memory of James Gray and Antony Dale, the two Brighton historians who helped me most during my early researches; also to John Barrow, photographer, who gave me hundreds of photographs over the years I knew him, including many he rescued during the famous 'clear out' at *The Argus* offices in Robert Street.

BY THE SAME AUTHOR

Brighton – The Century In Photographs Volume I
Brighton – The Century In Photographs Volume II
Brighton and Hove Then and Now Volume I
The Neat and Nippy Guide to Brighton's History

First published in 2003 by S B Publications
19 Grove Road, Seaford, East Sussex BN25 1TP
telephone: 01323 893498
fax: 01323 893860
email: sbpublications@tiscali.co.uk

© 2003 Christopher Horlock
The moral right of the author has been asserted
ISBN 185770 285 9

Typeset by JEMeditorial@aol.com
Printed by Pageturn Ltd, East Sussex, BN3 7EG.
Tel: (01273) 821500

ACKNOWLEDGEMENTS

As with Volume I, most of the photographs and prints come from my own collection, built up over many years and acquired from a great number of sources. Again though, several postcard collectors and historian colleagues have loaned supplementary material to 'enrich the mix', particularly Robert Jeeves of Step Back In Time (Queen's Road) and Philippe Garner, a noted collector. Staff at *The Argus* also allowed several pictures from their massive archive to be reproduced.

Tom Reeves of Lewes, as ever, did much of the copying work needed, often coming up with remarkable results from some pretty feeble source material.

Two of the most knowledgeable local historians there are – Trevor Povey of Portslade and Bob Elliston of Eastbourne – answered some really awkward questions without batting an eyelid. Peter Hill, windmill expert, gave information on West Blatchington Windmill, and Stephen Horlock (big brother) did the same for his famous cemetery in Lewes Road.

Most of the 1950s and 1960s intermediary views come from James Gray's popular *Changing Face* series, which ran in the *Brighton and Hove Herald* for more than 800 editions from 1953. He gave me virtually a complete duplicate set of these pictures and the 'modern' views, of course, are now half a century old and have historic interest themselves.

RENCES

est source material
k. These included
hich used to be the
, *Brighton and Hove*
A large number of
e always the first
figures about the
Hove.

riod guides (espe-
; also, *A Peep Into*
, by John George
); *Life In Brighton*,
vell Publications,
y Dale and James
rave New City
se, my extremely
f *Brighton* by Tim
1990).

king the modern,
straightforward,
e hundred views
ogged by traffic
double-parked in

front of buildings, adverse weather conditions, people giving me funny looks, etc, plus the sheer physical journeying from place to place and trying to park near the site needed, covering a vast area from Devil's Dyke to Black Rock. Phew!

Also, as before, the lens system used for pictures of the past often didn't equate at all with the cameras I used, meaning precise matching was nearly impossible. All in all, I've decided there definitely won't be a Volume III of this book!

CH

The Regent Cinema in Queen's Road, now the site of Boots the Chemist – see pages 48 and 49

George Bull's grocery store, North Street, 1875 (pages 46-47)

CONTENTS

A PLACE FOR EVERYTHING . . . .

History, it has been said, shows we learn nothing from history. Certainly in Brighton and Hove, the disastrous effect of placing buildings alongside others, where their scale or styles are totally at odds with one another, seems about to come round again – in a big way. The best (worst?) example from the past is obviously the block of flats on the Brighton Hove border known as Embassy Court, built in 1933-34. Everyone agrees now it should never have been built adjoining the eastern end of Brunswick Terrace, even though it's an important building of the so-called 'modern movement' and if anyone tried to demolish it there would probably be a huge outcry.

In 2003 we have similar proposals to install massive, state-of-the-art tower blocks on the King Alfred site in Hove, which although they may be intrinsically interesting ('crushed tin cans' is the less generous description), most feel the effect on the buildings and amenities around doesn't seem to have been considered.

As well as the contentious design (by Frank Gehry), the knock-on effect of several hundred more people suddenly living in this part of Hove causes equal concern. Which schools will their children go to? Has the car parking been properly addressed? What if a top storey caught fire? Have all the many other angles been thought out?

There's nothing wrong with outrageous buildings. The city of Brighton and Hove is full of them (thank goodness). The Royal Pavilion was considered completely over the top when first built. The Chain Pier of 1823 was extremely audacious when put forward as a rational project that would benefit Brighton. The church of St Bartholomew in Ann Street, when opened, was described as 'a monstrous excrescence'. Ah, but these are fairly small, outrageous buildings, I hear someone saying. Well what about the great squares and crescents that make up Kemp Town and Brunswick Town? These were built on a scale that dwarfs present day projects by miles. And these are among Brighton's most prized architectural possessions today. Brighton is well used to the absurd and extreme. Even the nudist beach – utterly condemned when first opened in 1980 – is now a Brighton institution.

Since the publication of Volume I of this book (in 2001) a lot of serious issues affecting the future of Brighton have come to a head. The collapse of the West Pier's concert hall and subsequent arson attacks have, for many, completely changed their view on the viability of its restoration. Plans for the station site saga, off London Road, remains contentious, so too are plans for a new football stadium for Brighton and Hove Albion. A scheme to run a monorail along the seafront from the Marina will, if it materialises, change the appearance of the seafront at a stroke.

Also, the publication of Anthony Seldon's book, *Brave New City*, not only threw down the gauntlet to all those

March 2003 – the West Pier in flames

actively responsible for shaping Brighton and Hove's future over the next decade or two, but also slapped a few faces with it first, admonishing those who seek to stand in the way of real progress by hanging on to old buildings at all costs.

History, of course, will judge all these views, plans and subsequent developments in its own way. It will also judge the motivations of those putting such ideas forward. But the early 2000s will be seen as an enormously vital period for the city, with some crucial decisions to be made about where the place is going and how it's going to get there. Seldon's book was the timely wake-up call the city needed.

The talk is for Brighton to get itself 'landmark' buildings. It already has them! The Royal Pavilion, St Bartholomew's church (higher than Westminster Abbey), the amazing curves of Brighton Station and Brighton Marina are just four. There are many others. If any new ones are to appear, they'd better be good! And tall isn't a defining element of a landmark building. Sussex Heights, the tallest structure in the city, is hardly a landmark.

What part does this book (and Volume I too) play in all this? It shows that, on a smaller scale, away from the grandiose, multi-million pound schemes currently in the pipeline, what a dreadful mess was made when some of the smaller sites of Brighton and Hove were redeveloped. Through monotonous, unimaginative design, corner-cutting or just plain 'profit first' scheming, some areas of the city have been reduced to an indifferent sterility; these areas needed just as much care in their redevelopment as anywhere else. Small should be beautiful.

Architects are God-like in the way they create environments they don't have to live with, but the common man (and woman) does. Page after page in this book shows once vital, vigorous buildings and streetscapes reduced to a boring, barren sameness. They can't come again. Those who allowed Embassy Court to be built right next to Brunswick Terrace are now castigated for perpetrating one of the worst planning decisions in Brighton and Hove's history. Castigate, too, those responsible for the smaller planning disasters seen in many of the pages that follow.

As said, there's nothing wrong with outrageous buildings (we really do need some), but their siting is the crucial factor. The trouble is that because Brighton and Hove are so developed there are few places where extravagant buildings can be sensibly positioned now, without them seeming both hemmed-in and overshadowing the past's more modest efforts already in place.

It would be nice if someone writing a similar book to this at the start of 2100 could say that, looking back, those responsible for planning new buildings for Brighton and Hove found there was 'a place for everything (maybe even those tin cans) but that everything was in its place'.

But then history shows that we learn nothing from history…

Christopher Horlock
October 2003

THE EASTERN BEACHES

We start this second volume of 'then and now' photographs on the seafront, with a view taken from the Palace Pier in the early 1890s. The pier was being built at this time, work starting in 1891. In the distance is the old Chain Pier, Brighton's first pier structure, opened in 1823.

The Palace Pier was built to replace the Chain Pier, but on a different site, closer to Old Steine. The Chain Pier blew down in a storm of 1896 and saved the Palace Pier company (which owned it) a huge demolition job, although claims for damages by individuals and firms who had property wrecked by the debris, as it battered the whole lower promenade area, held up work on the new pier for several years, delaying the opening until May 1899.

In the background runs the great sea wall, built to protect the chalk cliff from erosion by the sea. This massive enterprise, masterminded by William Lambert, took ten years to construct (completed in 1838 – the dates are on it but the plaque is very overgrown – small view) and is actually one of the

most extraordinary – and over-
looked - pieces of structural engineering in the whole city, being
nearly 200 years old.

In 2003, when the modern picture
was taken, many buildings in the
far distance remain the same, but
the beach profile has changed a
great deal. Madeira Walk and
Terraces, built between 1890 and
1897, occupy the mid-distance.

THE BEACH AND PALACE PIER

Another view of the early 1890s, taken from under the Palace Pier this time (still only partially built), again looking across to the Chain Pier.

The 2003 view shows a dramatic change to the height of the shingle and it's now impossible to stand where the old view was taken.

There's a plaque on the terracing above Madeira

"IN MEMORY" OLL CHAIIIPIER BRIGHTON

Drive marking the location of the Chain Pier and several relics are displayed on the Palace Pier (now called Brighton Pier, a name everyone chooses to ignore), including the two entrance booths, seen in the small picture of the entrance, and the old pier's signal cannon. When the pier was destroyed, the gates, also seen in the small view, found their way to front a house in Dyke Road Avenue, but are no longer there today.

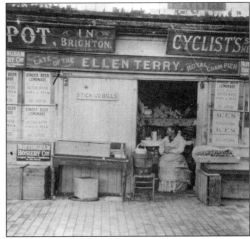

CHAIN PIER COTTAGES

Although the Chain Pier was destroyed in 1896, a cottage and several shops opposite the entrance survived until 1928, the date of the picture here. The cottage (the small building, just left of centre) was where the pier master had lived, with the neighbouring shops selling refreshments, novelties and Brighton souvenirs, the same as shops on the lower promenade do today. These buildings – collectively known for years as the Chain Pier Cottages – came down when the Aquarium (now the SeaLife Centre) was rebuilt and extended eastwards (which is taking place in the lower view, opposite) with modern shops built at the eastern end of the extension.

One curious aspect of these two older pictures is that the lamp standards on Marine Parade suddenly change. In 1928 'Greater Brighton' was created. This was when the boundary of Brighton was vastly extended to take in a huge amount of land surrounding the town, with places like North Moulsecoomb, Rottingdean, Ovingdean Patcham and part of Falmer, all becoming part of the Borough of Brighton. Celebrations and special

events were staged to mark this unique expansion of the town, including the upgrading of the lamps along the seafront.

The woman in the small view, in the doorway of one of the shops of Chain Pier Cottages, is Ellen Terry, who used to have a stall on the pier, situated inside one of its pylon-like arches. She lost her pitch when the pier blew down. The posters around her show she has ice cream, lemonade, soda, milk and ginger beer for sale. It's hard to make out what's in her basket – potatoes? Sausages?

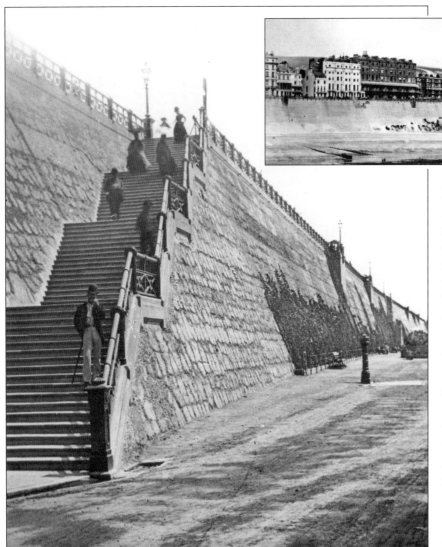

MADEIRA ROAD AND STEPS

Another view of the early 1890s, showing the steps leading down to Madeira Road (as it was called then) from Marine Parade, built when the massive sea wall was constructed. Then, of course, the steps led directly down to the beach.

The dark post in the middle distance is a water pump, used for watering the roads to keep dust down. In 1905 this road was the first in Brighton to receive a solid tarmac surface, in readiness for the speed trials initiated that year. The smaller view, top, gives a panoramic view of the sea wall, taken from the

14

Chain Pier in 1869. Madeira Road (Madeira Drive from 1905) did not exist until the early 1870s and huge banks of chalk and earth have been shored up against the wall's base, to prevent damage by the sea.

The corresponding 2003 picture still has the steps in place, but these are almost lost among the pillars and roof of the Aquarium Terraces. These and the adjoining Madeira Walk terracing – built in the 1890s (small view, opposite) – have proved to be an ideal 'grandstand' over the years for many of the events held on Madeira Drive, including the Stock Exchange walk (from 1903), the speed trials (from 1905), the British Heart Foundation Bike Ride (from 1976) and the London to Brighton Veteran Car Rally (first held in 1896, but not at first on this part of the seafront).

VOLK'S ELECTRIC RAILWAY

This, the oldest surviving railway of its kind in the world, opened in 1883 and first ran from opposite the Aquarium to the Chain Pier (there was no Palace Pier then). It proved so popular that the line was extended to the Banjo Groyne (where the train sheds are today) and in 1901 it was lengthened again to Black Rock. Part of the new route ran over the sea, as seen in the view of about 1905. This gave passengers an unexpected thrill once over the Banjo Groyne and probably was accompanied by a few gasps of terror as the sea appeared under their feet.

The view taken in 2003 shows the elevated part of the track gone due to the eventual build-up of shingle on this part of the beach. At present, there are concerns that plans to run a monorail along the seafront, from the Marina to Shoreham, will force the closure of Volk's Railway, which celebrated 120 years of service on Brighton's seafront in 2003.

The old advertisement for the railway, seen below, dates from the 1890s.

CONCERT PARTY ON THE BEACH

Crowds on the lower promenade and beach enjoying a concert party show given from an improvised theatre roughly opposite the Grand Hotel. The date is the early 1900s and the group are the Highwaymen, founded by singer Frank Gomm in 1905. Gomm took the stage name Jack Sheppard (after the famous highwayman) and he continued performing on Brighton's seafront right up to World War II using this pseudonym. He died in 1968, aged ninety-four.

Gomm's main claim to fame was discovering Tom Walls, now a largely forgotten British film actor, and also Brighton's own Max Miller, who became the top stand-up comedian in the country during the 1930s, the war years and the 1950s, performing in three Royal Variety Shows and making a number of films.

In 2003 (the view here shows the redeveloped lower promenade) concert parties are a thing of the past, although one or two nostalgic 'old-style' shows are staged during the annual Brighton Festival. There are still all kinds of off-beat entertainment to be found intermittently on the beach esplanade – the most famous event (or is it infamous?) of recent years being Fatboy Slim's rock concert, where thousands descended on Brighton's beaches for a free pop gig in July 2002.

BRIGHTON FISHMARKET

A view of the 1920s now, taken on the hard between the piers, where Brighton's fishmarket operated until 1960. In the distance is the Winter Garden on the Palace Pier, opened in April 1912.

For many centuries, Brighton fishermen sold much of what they caught straight off the beach. During the 1840s some rented stalls in a building in nearby Market Street, but in 1867 the first purpose-built arches, on the lower promenade area, were opened for them to trade from. These were rebuilt in 1885-86 (seen on the left of the old view) and the market formed something of a tourist attraction, particularly when auctions were taking place. However, by the late 1950s, with the number of fishermen dwindling, the market arches were considered out of date and unhygienic, so the council closed them, those fishermen left having to move to new premises in Circus Street. In 1974, the old market arches were demolished (below, left) and replaced by the modern buildings housing amusement arcades and shops, seen in the 2003 view. Despite the opening of the nearby fishing museum in May 1994, (below, right) it really was the end of an era.

OLD SHIP HOTEL

Up now on to King's Road and an 1890s view of the city's oldest hotel, the Old Ship, which dates back to at least the sixteenth century, but has obviously been rebuilt since then, several times.

By the late 1700s the Old Ship had become the town's most celebrated coaching hostelry, but was also used to hold meetings for town business, and as a magistrates' court

from time to time. In 1795 a court-martial was held at the hotel resulting in two local militiamen receiving the death penalty for mutiny. The hotel was at the height of its popularity during the early 1800s, in the wake of the Prince of Wales' residency at the nearby Royal Pavilion. This was when the Old Ship was the place to be seen and fashionable visitors crowded its assembly rooms for dancing, concerts, card games and gossip.

The Old Ship features in the classic novel *Vanity Fair* by William Thackeray (inset), published in serial form,

during 1847-48. He wrote a large part of it while staying at the hotel, and made Brighton the town where his two main characters (George and Amelia) stay following their marriage. Charles Dickens was another celebrated guest. In 1831 the virtuoso violinist Niccolo Paganini gave a concert in the hotel assembly rooms (which are still there). His fee was fifty guineas, which stunned the promoter, but Paganini later took great pleasure in giving most of it back.

In 2003 the building stands much enlarged and altered but, due to its enormous age, is still the most important and historic hotel in Brighton and Hove.

BEDFORD HOTEL

One of Brighton's lost seafront buildings is seen in the old picture here of about 1880. This is the elegant Bedford Hotel, which opened in 1829, only a few years after the Royal Pavilion was completed. Like Bedford Square and Bedford Street, it was almost certainly named after the Duke of Bedford, who stayed a number of times at Brunswick Square during the 1820s.

The Bedford's most famous guest was Charles Dickens, opposite, who wrote much of *Dombey and Son* while staying there. When the Royal Pavilion was closed in 1845, members of the royal family, when visiting Brighton, invariably stayed at the Bedford.

In April 1964 a fire broke out at the hotel resulting in the death of two people. Despite only the uppermost storeys being gutted, it was decided the whole building should come

down, and the grey slab tower that stands on the site today opened in September 1967. In 2003, it bears the name of Hilton Brighton West Pier Hotel and any number of people have derided this building. Anthony Seldon, in *Brave New City*, says; 'It would be hard to find a starker contrast any-where of the beautiful being replaced by the gross. View it from any angle and one cannot discover a single redeeming feature. In every sense, a disgrace.'

RUSSELL STREET

An amazing contrast between old and new pictures here. The view on the opposite page was taken half way up Russell Street in April 1968. This street, built up from the 1780s, no longer exists. It ran from King's Road to Upper Russell Street, which was at right angles to it. Upper Russell Street then curved northwards to Western Road, coming out opposite Queen Square.

The large building dominating the picture is the Cannon Brewery which was opened in 1821 by brewer John Barnett, who first made beer in his Russell Street house and sold it round the streets from a handcart. It must have been good as it led to the building of the brewery, which was very large and would have employed a great many people, plus the eventual ownership of fifty pubs. Brewing ceased in 1929, when owned by Tamplins, who ran it then as just a bottling plant. Closure came in 1965 for the Churchill Square development. Russell Street and the remains of the brewery came down as late as 1969 (when Churchill Square was already up and running – it opened in October 1968). Note that top right, the Spirit of Brighton sculpture can be seen in the distance, a feature of the original square. The present, rebuilt Churchill Square opened in September 1998.

The site of Russell Street was eventually partially occupied by the £10 million Brighton Centre, which opened in September 1977. In the comparative view, which roughly approximates with the street scene, a temporary ice-rink is being installed for the annual *Holiday On Ice* show, first seen at the centre in 1978. In 2003, there are plans to redevelop the Brighton Centre, remodel the exterior and upgrade its facilities.

SEAFRONT HOTELS

More hotels are seen in this 1920s view of King's Road at the corner of Black Lion Street (centre). The shop on the left would be demolished when the Old Ship Hotel was extended in 1963-64. Right of centre is the Exeter Hotel, and far right is the Hollywood Hotel, both popular middle-of-the-range hotels for holidaymakers for several decades.

   After World War II, these hotels become council offices (seen below) and then were demolished in the 1980s for the huge Ramada Hotel, now the Thistle presently on the site, with a civic centre behind for the council. The small view below shows the hotel being built in March 1986.

ROYAL ALBION HOTEL

Moving to the corner of Old Steine now and a view of another of the city's historic hotels, the Royal Albion. Previously on the site was a seaside mansion known for a while as Russell House, seen in the drawing, which was the residence of Dr Richard Russell (inset), who published his very serious paper on the benefits of sea bathing in 1750. This brought crowds of wealthy invalids flocking to the town to try the sea-water cure, and forced Brighton to lay on its early resort facilities, including ballrooms, a theatre, library and racecourse.

The plaque on the southern side of the hotel says that Russell lived in the house from 1759. Oh dear – that was actually the year

he died. One day someone will change it. After serving a number of uses, including being the seasonal residence of the Duke of Cumberland (with whom the young Prince of Wales would stay on his first visit to the town in 1783), a school, then something called Haine's Toy Repository and Puppet Theatre, the house was demolished and the Albion Hotel opened on the site in August 1826. Arnold Bennett wrote his novel *Clayhanger* while staying at the hotel in 1910. In 1913, when very run down, it was restored by the dynamic Harry Preston who enticed many literary, sporting and artistic celebrities to stay at the hotel including, in the summer of 1925, Jack Dempsey, heavyweight boxing champion of the world. More recently, in 1998, there was a huge fire at the hotel and some £7 million was spent on restoration. The Royal Albion is another of Brighton's famous hotels just saturated in history.

OLD STEINE

Next, a really ancient photograph taken in Old Steine. It's sometime in the 1860s and the view looks east towards St James's Street (in the background), with the statue of George IV in its original place, where the war memorial now stands (behind the horse). First put up in October 1828, this statue by Francis Chantrey is now at the bottom of Church Street, at the northern end of the Pavilion grounds.

The picture shows a horse cab waiting for a customer. A top-hatted policeman has obligingly entered the frame, so we see what Brighton policemen looked like 143 years ago.

The thirty-ton statue was moved to the bottom of Church Street in March 1922, so the war memorial could be built, still on the site today. The small view here shows it being moved, a large steam tractor pulling it the short distance northwards.

In 1927, numbers thirteen, fourteen and fifteen North Parade – immediately behind the statue in the old photograph, were demolished and replaced by a Lyons restaurant. The comparative 2003 view has its background detail almost obliterated by the trees, which were hardly noticeable in the old picture.

CASTLE SQUARE AND HANNINGTONS STORE

Moving into the Old Town area of Brighton now, the photographer who took this early 1920s picture was standing in Castle Square, with East street running off to the left and North Street directly ahead of him. The large corner shop is occupied by Treachers, a library and stationers, and the photograph was obviously taken to record the building before it was demolished. In 1845 Treachers leased this corner site from Hanningtons, which had its own shops on either side. In 1924 the lease ran out and the shop was cleared to unite most of Hanningtons into one large, L-shaped store.

Hanningtons first opened for business in July 1808, at 3 North Street, managed by Smith Hannington. His first shop is seen in the small view. The firm lasted – with greatly expanded premises – for nearly 200 years, closing in June 2001. The Hannington family was connected with the store until 1966. A lively history of what was Brighton and Hove's largest ever department store, written by Sidonie Bond, was published in 2002.

In the 2003 picture, the corner site is being redeveloped to make units of separate shops inside the shell of Hanningtons' old premises.

EAST STREET

A really old photograph of East Street, looking south to the corner of Bartholomews, dating from about 1860. Amazingly, the modern view of 2003, taken some 140 years later, is little changed. The rounded corner building survives, as does the whole scale and topography of the street, almost certainly the oldest in the city. It's probably the state of the road that catches the eye most; then it was most likely made up of crushed stone and earth. No road in Brighton or Hove would receive a tarmac surface until 1905.

After taking the old view here, the photographer moved his camera down East Street and positioned it near the rounded building but facing the Town Hall.

The smaller view shows the picture he then took. It's very rare to find a pair of old pictures taken within minutes of each other, in this way.

Brighton's Town Hall had stood for only twenty-nine years when these pictures were taken. When its foundation stone was laid in April 1830, George IV was still King of England.

ROYAL JUBILEE CELEBRATION

A more modern view of East Street now, looking in the opposite direction from the picture on page 36, with the entrance gate to the Royal Pavilion estate clearly visible in the background, across Castle Square. Decorations have been put up to celebrate the Silver Jubilee of King George V and Queen Mary, which took place in May 1935. Similar bunting was in place in many other streets of the town, including Castle Square, North Street, West Street, the Clock Tower area and Western Road. Trafalgar Street was also decorated, but not it seems, Church Street or North Road.

Notice the unusual traffic sign on the left of this photograph, stating 'no waiting this side on odd dates'. The 2003 views shows some changes to East Street, the main one being the way it's become pedestrianised with a taxi rank area, formed in 1990.

NORTH STREET

Back to North Street now and a view of the early 1900s with the familiar Hanningtons store in the distance, and another large building opposite (built 1879), which has 'Academy of Music' just under the roof line; for many years this was an electrical store. It juts out, causing North Street to narrow significantly between Princes Place and Castle Square. This bottleneck didn't cause huge problems at the

time the picture was taken, as there was little traffic and two horse-drawn carts or buses could probably just about pass each other in the gap. However, by the 1920s, the narrowing was causing problems for motor buses (introduced to the town early in 1904), cars, delivery vans and lorries, so that in 1930 the building was taken down to ease traffic congestion.

The smaller view (opposite) shows the site in the 1960s, the one here is another of 2003, with few changes between these last two.

COUNTESS OF HUNTINGDON'S CHURCH

A little further up North Street now and one of this street's most significant buildings is seen in very different forms over the years. This is the Countess of Huntingdon's Church, which saw many rebuildings over its 200 years of life.

Selina, Countess of Huntingdon, wife of the ninth Earl, had come to Brighton in 1755 hoping the sea air would help the ailing health of her son – who later died of smallpox. She lived in a substantial house in what would now be The Lanes area, behind North Street. She was a fervent Methodist, but there being no church for her and others of similar faith in Brighton, she opened a small chapel in her own garden (backing on to North Street) in 1761, financing it by selling some of her jewels, to the value of nearly £700. Significant preachers who took services made her chapel popular and it was soon too small to hold the increasing numbers wishing to attend. It was enlarged in 1767, then again, in Greek style, in 1774, seen in the main photograph, which dates from 1868. At a service in 1851 it is known 1,100 people were present. Once up and running, other churches of the Countess of Huntingdon's 'connexion' (as it became known) were built in other towns. A second one in Brighton was built in Ann Street, in 1830, but later this became Congregational.

The North Street church was demolished and rebuilt in enlarged form again in 1870, with a spire on its east side, seen opposite about 1890. This had a galleried interior and

now held around 1,500 people.

Its central location in the town saw it flourish for many years, but by the 1960s time had taken its toll on the building and it became unsafe, closing in September 1966. The tower began to tilt and had to be taken down in 1968. The main body of the church went in 1972 and a plaque inside the doorway of the modern building occupying the site (the 2003 view) is all that's left marking a unique building in Brighton's diverse religious affairs.

SALEM BAPTIST CHAPEL IN BOND STREET

A glance down Bond Street in the early 1970s, from the North Street end, would have taken in another church building, the Salem Baptist Chapel, seen in this view, shortly before it was demolished in 1974. Built in 1861 to designs by Thomas Simpson, the chapel replaced an earlier one on the site, dating back as far as 1787. The chapel seen here closed in 1971, when the minister, the Reverend Ernest Carter, emigrated to South Africa.

The building was replaced by the shops and offices in the 2003 view.

PRINCES CINEMA

Returning to North Street again, the southern side, and yet another building that no longer stands – the Princes Cinema. This picture house, first opened in 1911 as the Bijou Empire, operated under a variety of names and was rebuilt several times. The view here is of the early 1930s, when it was the Princes, its name from 1915. It would become the Brighton Film Theatre between 1969 and 1978 and close as Cinescene in June 1983. The 2003 picture shows the fast-food store that the building became (in 1988), although, inside, the screen and some cinema equipment remain.

JUNCTION OF NORTH STREET AND WEST STREET

Moving further up North Street to where it meets West Street, we see George Bull's large grocery shop, about 1875, with its distinctive, curved frontage. This had been built during the 1850s, on the site of a smaller store (taken over by Bull),

which probably went up following the sale of a house on the site, in 1794.

This shop was the first building to come down for the long job of widening West Street, on its western side, starting in 1925, but taking until 1963, when the George Hotel, just off the bottom, seafront end of West Street, was demolished. World War II interrupted the widening and rebuilding work, as it did much redevelopment in Brighton at the time.

The very first shop to open in North Street is always said to have been in 1757 by Ambrose Austin (its exact location isn't known) who, according to his advertisement in the *Lewes Journal* sold, 'all sorts of dressed Hemp and Flax, all sorts of Groceries, all sorts of New and Second Hand Cloaths, Hats, Stockings, Shoes Boots and Clogs'. Three years after Austin's shop opened for trading, the Countess of Huntingdon's first chapel opened, detailed on the previous pages.

THE REGENT CINEMA

Turning right from North Street into Queen's Road, we see Brighton's most famous lost cinema, the Regent, in the early 1960s, occupying a site where the large Boots the Chemist store now stands, built in 1979, opposite the Clock Tower.

The Regent opened in July, 1921, and was the first – and most would say the best – of Brighton's large 'super cinemas'. The architect was Robert Atkinson, who toured America for several months studying state-of-the-art cinemas before designing the Regent for Brighton. The final cost was more than £400,000, an astonishing sum for any entertainment building in 1921. Much of this went on massive excavations to provide an underground dance hall, which was ultimately abandoned but added to the roof, opening in 1923. Initially, the seating capacity of the cinema was to be 2,200, but this was increased to 3,000.

The first film was *A Yankee At The Court Of King Arthur*, supported by Pathe Gazette shorts. In the first ten days of operating, the Regent attracted

more than 100,000 patrons.

The other view here, of 1962, shows the corner of North Street and Queen's Road looking directly north, with the Regent in the mid-distance on the right. The large corner building was once the White Lion Hotel, dating from 1874. Later, an early Virgin music store would open in the large shop on the ground floor of this building and a young Richard Branson could be found serving behind the counter. The Regent closed in 1973 and mostly came down the following year for the Boots building, seen in the modern 2003 view.

ODD FELLOWS HALL

The eastern side of Queen's Road is seen now, just past Church Street where the Odd Fellows Hall used to be.

The Odd Fellows were a charitable, fraternal organisation, providing mutual aid for members, as well as help for poor and needy folk in the area. The first solid evidence of Odd Fellow groups operating in Britain is in London, in 1748. Manchester was a very prominent early centre as well. The unusual name seems to derive from the widely differing 'odd' trades of the members that formed the first groups.

The building here, to house the Brighton branch, was built by a John Fabian in 1853, through donations and fund-raising. The foundation stone – still in place on the office block that occupies the site today – was laid by the Chief Constable of Brighton, H B Tamplin. (no doubt connected with Tamplins, the well-known local brewers somewhere along the line). The hall was officially opened in June, 1854.

There were separate lodge meetings for men, women and children, which took place on the ground floor. There were billiard tables in the basement and dance evenings, which were sometimes open to the public, were held in the upper hall. The children's lodge would have been run along the lines of a youth club, and met once a month. For small weekly contributions, assistance was given with doctors' and dentists' fees (there being no National Health Service until 1948), funeral costs and financial matters such as insurance cover.

Medicals were held in this hall for men about to serve in World War II. These were pretty embarrassing as sometimes it was a female doctor examining recruits who were just seventeen years old. The check-up was very basic: a specimen had to be produced, then 'bend over', 'cough', 'can you hear what I'm whispering to you?' etc, plus the reading of an eye chart. There was an aptitude test afterwards that involved taking a door lock apart and fitting it together again, then a test involving basic arithmetic and writing skills.

Once the NHS was set up, after the war, the Odd Fellows' role in assisting with health care was reduced, but other support work continued. The building was sold for redevelopment, quite why is a bit of a mystery (probably too big to maintain) and the old photograph here dates from June 1964, five years before demolition. Despite this, the Odd Fellows continue to flourish in the Brighton and Hove area.

The 2003 view shows the dreary office block that replaced the historic 1854 hall.

BRIGHTON, HOVE AND PRESTON DISPENSARY

Moving further up Queen's Road, to where it meets North Road (left), we have a building that was for many years the Brighton and Hove Dispensary (the 'Preston' bit was later dropped), founded with the intention of 'assisting the sick poor with advice and medicine'. Although this had started in 1809 in Nile Street, the fund didn't move to these premises, specially built for them, until 1849. The way health schemes operated then probably applied to obtaining medicines here. Contributions would be asked for, determined by how well off the sick person was. Those who could afford the full price had to

pay it, others gave only something towards the cost. The really poor received their medicines and advice free. After operating for nearly a century, the old dispensary closed in 1948 and was renamed Churchill House, after war-time Prime Minister, Winston Churchill. Financed by donations, it became headquarters for the many regimental groups and ex-service organisations that were now caring for those who fought in the war. Later an insurance firm opened offices on the ground floor, but the building was eventually another casualty of 1960s 'progress' and was replaced by the nondescript offices seen in the 2003 view.

QUEEN'S ROAD

An extremely rare view of Queen's Road now, looking from the corner of Upper Gloucester Road (right), towards the station. The date must be 1877, when Queen's Road was widened on its eastern side, hence the lack of buildings on the right, with construction work screened by the advertisement hoardings. The station, which should be straight ahead, is lost in the mist.

The decorative arch means someone important was visiting the town (arriving by train) and in this case it was the Lord Mayor of London, who came on a state visit to dedicate to public use the widened Queen's Road.

The modern view of 2003 shows the corner building (left) still in place but the buildings that went up following the widening have all now been replaced with a really 'mixed bag' of offices and shops in a variety of modern styles and scales that don't complement each other at all.

THE RAILWAY STATION

Up to Brighton Station now and a clear view of about 1908 showing all sorts fascinating detail, including a fine assortment of lamps on the left. At the time of this view, shops, pubs and business premises ran right up to the station building. The Terminus Hotel (small picture) was the last building before the station on the western side, demolished in 1926 when Junction Road was formed. This was widened in 1935, losing more of the property in Queen's Road seen here.

The clock in the centre is on the roof of the original terminus building, dating back to 1840. Six companies petitioned Parliament in 1836 to build a railway from London to Brighton. The chosen one was the Direct Line planned by Sir John Rennie. The first trains from London to Brighton ran in September 1841. The company architect, David Moccatta, designed the station, with the huge glass-covered roof, arching up behind the original frontage (and spoiling the look of it) added in 1882-83. A canopy in front of the building was also added some twenty years later (so pretty new at the time of the old picture) obliterating the front of the original design and spoiling it a lot more.

WEST STREET

Returning to the Old Town area now; a view of West Street, looking north, taken about 1920. This gives a good view of the western side (left) before extensive demolition took place, starting in 1925, to widen the street (see pages 46-47).

The vicarage of St Paul's Church is the house on the left where the railings and steps are. This was demolished in 1932. The sign for the Academy Cinema, opened in 1911, can be made out on the far right, just above the turning into Boyces Street.

The small view of the 1960s shows the widened street with the new buildings that went up during the late 1920s and 1930s in place, but built further back on a new building line (so the Clock Tower can now be seen). The vicarage has gone and the Academy stands rebuilt (in the 1930s).

The third, 2003 picture, shows few changes to the actual buildings,

but for some, their usage has changed dramatically; previous financial institutions are now restaurants and bars. The Academy has long since gone, closing in 1973, the same year as the Regent.

KING'S HEAD INN

West Street again, but lower down, and a much earlier picture; this view is about 1880. St Paul's Church, in the hazy distance, was built in 1846-47, the spire added in the 1870s. The low building in the centre, right of the ladder, is the King's Head Inn. Back in the 1600s the George Inn stood on this site, the hostelry where the future Charles II supposedly met Brighton boat owner Nicholas Tettersall, in October 1651. Charles had lost the Battle of Worcester during the final skirmishes of the Civil War and needed to flee the country to avoid a fate similar to that of his father Charles I, who had been executed by order of

Parliament in 1649. Tettersall took him from Shoreham to Fécamp and temporary exile until the restoration of the monarchy in 1660. This event has been celebrated each year, since 1977, by the Royal Escape Yacht Race, where some eighty yachts race between Shoreham and Fécamp in Normandy, a distance of sixty-eight nautical miles.

The site of the King's Head is now, in 2003, the £7 million Quality Hotel, which opened in September 1991 as the Oak Hotel, a more appropriate name as it linked with the history of the site – King Charles hid in an oak tree to escape capture following defeat at Worcester. This hotel was formerly the location of the well-known SS Brighton, a 1934 swimming stadium that became an ice rink and home to the famed Brighton Tigers ice hockey team.

DUKE STREET

Through to Duke Street now and a shop on the eastern side, number 32, owned by T Roles, 'Practical Engraver', photographed in 1889. A strange-looking tandem is on show for some reason. The site was once the location for a theatre, the town's second playhouse (below) which saw performances from July 1790 until November 1806. It then moved to new, larger premises in New Road and is still operating today as the Theatre Royal. The Duke Street site became a large private house (with a front garden) which

was converted into the shop – Roles being one of the subsequent owners. The mid-1960s view, right, shows the shop site occupied by IT Office Equipment; today (2003) the Havana restaurant is there.

WIDENING OF DUKE STREET
The corner of Duke Street (right) and Middle Street (left) in 1868. Duke Street had been widened the previous year on its northern side, leaving trees, previously growing between the houses and shops, standing in what was now the new road. The picture shows them about to be removed, before new property went up along the now widened roadway. An advertisement on the corner shop shows a dozen bottles of port costing 15/- (75p today).

On the extreme left of the old view Middle Street School can be seen, the city's oldest school, founded in 1805. This will be 200 years old in 2005, making it one of the oldest schools of its kind in the country.

The 2003 picture shows the corner building still in place, with the curve of the road turning down Duke Street, the upper part of which was pedestrianised early in 1983, although it wasn't formally inaugurated until two years later.

65

NORTH STREET COTTAGES

A row of houses known as North Street Cottages is seen here, in the 1930s. They were probably the best part of 100 years old when this picture was taken. These homes stood in the Lanes area, just behind Brighton Place, off a bend in Meeting House Lane. By the 1930s these five cottages were considered slum property and demolished as such not long after the picture was taken. It wasn't until the early 1960s that the site of the terrace became one of the low entrances to the new Brighton Square, with shops on the northern (left) side, seen in the 2003 view. The smaller picture, of November 1961, shows work on redeveloping the central part of The Lanes area in progress. The view looks down Meeting House Lane towards North Street. Brighton Square, with its twenty-four shops and fifteen flats, opened in 1966 and was described by Clifford Musgrave in *Life in Brighton* as 'one of the most imaginative and delightful improvements carried out in Brighton in the whole of its history'.

Today the development is considered just a bit dated and the ecstatic praise heaped on it at the time was mostly due to the realisation that all other 1960s projects, including Churchill Square, were going to be awful, concrete slab affairs, among the *worst* improvements in the whole of its history.

NEW ROAD

New Road is seen now, a copy of a postcard view of the early 1900s, with a policeman managing to dominate the whole picture. The frontage of the Theatre Royal, with its octagonal turrets, dates from 1894, although the theatre is much older, opening in 1807. On the right is the western wall of the Pavilion grounds. The railings here would be removed in 1937. Some of the trees were felled in 1982, others came down during the hurricane of 1987. The buildings in the distance, in Church Street, were demolished in the early 1970s, and the site has stood empty for thirty years.

DOME COTTAGE

The eastern side of New Road now and a view of the early 1900s showing an ivy-covered house that was demolished in 1932. This was Dome Cottage (numbered 29a New Road), once part of stabling that existed on the site, said to be for the exclusive use of Mrs Fitzherbert, the illegal wife of George IV, builder of the Royal Pavilion. After her death in 1837 the stable buildings served a number of uses over the years, including housing the town's fire brigade. During the 1890s the cottage was lived in by the man seen in the photograph, F W Brown, works superintendent of the Royal Pavilion estate. His wife stands with him by their doorway. They brought up five children in the cottage, two sons and three daughters. The 2003 view shows the Pavilion Theatre built on the site in 1937. This was when the interior of the Dome was reconstructed and turned into a concert hall with further amenities created, including this small theatre.

Just out of sight on the left of the modern view is one of the original houses of New Road – in use as the booking office for the Dome – built in the early 1820s.

CHURCH STREET

An unrecognisable picture of Church Street just above Gardner Street. It's early 1938 and old shops are being demolished, probably for road widening. Any proposed redevelopment of the site would have been put on hold by the outbreak of World

War II. As it turned out, the site was left derelict for several decades (see next page) and substantial widening of the road similarly delayed.

CHURCH STREET

Church Street again, looking west from the corner of Bond Street (left) in February 1960. The shops cleared on the previous page stood in the gap opposite the lorry. Between Bread Street and Tichborne Street is the 1805 Providence Chapel, which closed in 1965 and came down the same year so the road could be widened. The parishioners moved to a church in West Hill Road.

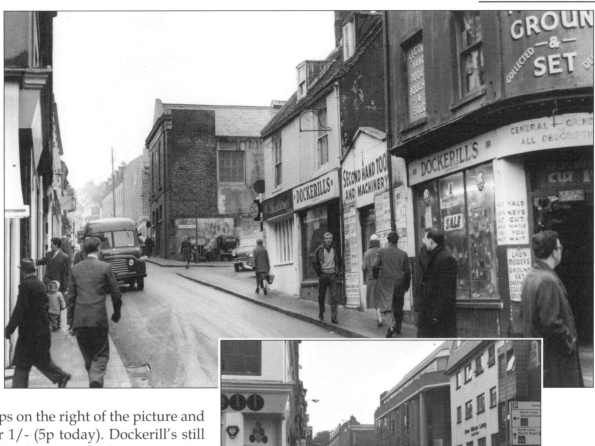

Dockerill's, the ironmongers, founded in 1905, occupy several shops on the right of the picture and a sign offers keys cut for 1/- (5p today). Dockerill's still trades in Church Street; the firm acquired new premises on the other side of the road, below Bond Street, in 1980. It's hard to believe that narrow Church Street carried two-way traffic until 1976.

BREAD STREET

Bread Street, seen below from the Church Street end in 1937, no longer exists. Once it was almost entirely residential (as were most other streets in the area). The houses and shop here were demolished in 1945 so that electricity works, then in North Road, could be expanded.

The building in the distance – seen better in the smaller 1959 view - is the church of St Mary Magdalene, opened in

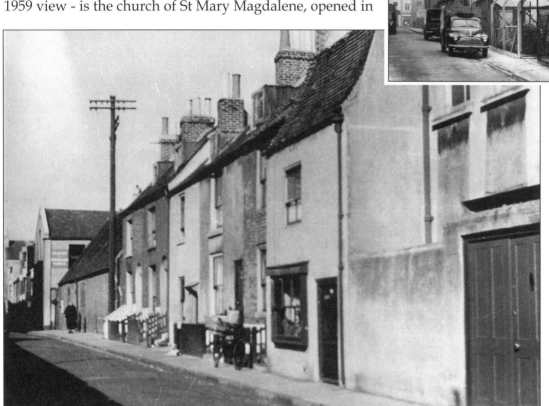

October 1862. The interest with this church, which was never consecrated for some reason, is that it was the first to be financed by the Reverend Arthur Douglas Wagner who, with his father, was responsible for eleven churches in Brighton, including St Martin's in Lewes Road, St Paul's in West Street and the truly spectacular St Bartholomew's in Ann Street. This Bread Street church, which could hold 700 people, closed in 1948, with the electricity board using the building (probably for storage) until 1965. What was left of

Bread Street was lost in 1989-1990 when the International Factors building went up at the corner of Tichborne Street, part of which is seen in the 2003 view.

Between Bread Street and Gardner Street once stood a maze of small streets and courtyards built in the early 1800s. Here, in 1826, in the slum street known as Pimlico (where more than 650 people were living in the 1860s) the great prize fighter Tom Sayers was born (inset). He became a champion boxer before the Queensberry Rules were set up and boxing matches were bare-knuckle bouts, where the fight continued with no set number of rounds and contestants kept pounding away until one gave up or was knocked out. Sayers' first professional fight, for £5, lasted just twelve minutes. In a later contest, for £100 and the middleweight championship title, Sayers lost – after sixty-one rounds. This was the only defeat of his career. Often training at the Plough Inn, Rottingdean, Sayers went for the heavyweight title in 1857 against The Tipton Slasher (William Perry) for a purse of £200. This fight lasted one hour, forty-two minutes. Another notable contest was the first ever international bout with the American John Heenan – declared a draw after thirty-seven rounds. Sayers died in 1865 from a pretty hefty combination of pneumonia, TB, diabetes and a collapsed lung. His funeral at Highgate Cemetery in London was attended by some 10,000 people.

Pimlico and other surrounding hovels were swept away in the 1870s and Titchborne Street was built over the site.

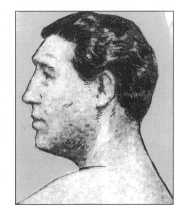

REGENT IRON AND BRASS FOUNDRY

Through to North Road now and two important industrial premises near the top of the street, on the northern side, pho-tographed in the 1860s. The Regent Iron and Brass Foundry, established about 1815, dominates the view (from which Foundry Street nearby takes its name). The towers for the Chain Pier (seen on pages 8-11) were cast here. It also pro-

duced the bridges over Trafalgar Street and New England Road, railings for The Level, Queen's Park and the Victoria Gardens (all gone now) plus hundreds of drain and coal-hole covers for use throughout the town. The foundry had two large beam steam engines, and employed more than 100 people, It operated suc-cessfully for near-ly a century, one of its last orders being railings for the racecourse, but the firm went bankrupt and closed in 1912.

Further down is the engineering premises of Palmer and Company, who were in North Road between 1845 and 1904. In the 1820s, gas fittings were made here to light the Royal Pavilion.

The 2003 view shows the replacement building, the Post Office premises, which took some three years to build, open-ing in November 1926 at a cost of some £8,000. A telephone exchange opened in the building a year later.

KENSINGTON GARDENS

Kensington Gardens now, seen about 1905 and still gas-lit, judging from the lamps and lamp standards on view. The photograph looks towards Gloucester Road, with some properties (left) still private houses at this time.

Kensington Gardens (like Spring Gardens) takes it name from extensive market gardens that once lay along the whole northern side of North Road, when it was the northern boundary of the town. Kensington Gardens was developed from about 1808 and it was the first street to be built northwards from North Road, those either side of it coming later. Gloucester Road was built up in the 1840s.

Today (2003) Kensington Gardens remains one of the most quirky and attractive shopping thoroughfares in the North Laine area, its popularity due partly to it being traffic-free.

The modern view here is dominated by Theobald House, the high-rise flats in the distance, built in 1964 (small view).

GLOUCESTER PLACE

The bottom of North Road is seen here, about 1890, where some very attractive houses, numbers 1-4 Gloucester Place, used to stand. Built about 1800, they were a superb example of a small Regency-style terrace. But the tide of 1930s progress in Brighton saw them demolished in 1934 and replaced by a telephone exchange building, taking over from the one in North Road. This was known as

Telephone House, a huge building completely out of scale with everything else around it (small view). This developed structural faults and came down in 1982-83 and Trustcard House, seen in the 2003 view, was subsequently built on the site, opening in 1985.

RICHMOND PLACE

Across to nearby Richmond Place and a terrace of houses, which stood opposite the top of St Peter's church grounds, known as Waterloo Place. Half of the terrace is seen in this 1960 view before the site was redeveloped. Yes, the name derives from the famous battle of 1815. The terrace was built about 1818 by Amon Wilds, a Lewes builder, and designed by his son, Amon Henry Wilds. The latter, in partnership with Charles Busby, built most of the great Regency crescents and squares in Brighton, including the entire Kemp Town estate and a huge number of fine houses in places like Marine Parade, Marine Square, Portland Place and Regency Square. Busby lived at 11 Waterloo Place for about seven years until 1830.

The houses seen on the previous page were demolished between 1968 and 1970 and replaced by a truly awful building, Wellesley House (2003 view). Number 9, the last to go, was occupied by eighty-nine-year-old Harriet Sylvester, who wouldn't move out. The new office block was built either side of her home and completed after her death in 1974 when the house could be demolished.

THE 1987 HURRICANE

A picture where it isn't redevelopers responsible for the destruction of an area, but the weather. On October 16, 1987, southern England was hit by a spectacular hurricane, when wind speeds of more than 100mph were recorded. The storm startled everyone with its suddenness and massive destructive force. Warning signs had started when the New Barn area of Rottingdean was inundated with mud washed down by torrential rain from nearby fields. In the next few days the depression over the country deepened, resulting in the south being subjected to Force 10 winds that caused unprecedented damage the length and breadth of Sussex. The worst was how effortlessly the storm tore down trees, with all parks and public gardens completely devastated. Across the southern part of England some fifteen million trees were lost (six million in Sussex alone), three million people were left without power and there were nineteen deaths.

In Brighton, on The Level, seen here, 323 trees were uprooted with another thirty-seven so badly damaged they were later felled and burnt (small view).

Only 150 were left standing. Most had been planted in 1844, when The Level was first laid out.

The 2003 view shows many of the saplings planted after the storm beginning to mature.

The last time trees were uprooted in any number during a storm in Brighton had been in November 1924. Trees came down in the Pavilion grounds and Preston Park, windows were shattered on the seafront and damage was done to the Palace Pier and Volk's Railway.

THE KING AND QUEEN HOTEL

Marlborough Place is the location now, looking south, with the King and Queen Hotel in the background and tram rails being installed, putting the date of 1901 on this view. Trams ran in Brighton between 1901 and 1939, when they were withdrawn and replaced by trolley buses.

The King and Queen was probably first built during the reign of George II. Early in 1931, when the building seen in the old photograph was under reconstruction, coins of his reign (1727-1760) were found among the foundations. The new hotel, with its mock-Tudor appearance (which was then in fashion and given to many properties, including houses), opened in 1932.

SUSSEX STREET

Next, our photographs move into an area that has been dubbed 'backstreet Brighton'; this is Sussex Street, photographed in 1928, with just one car in sight. The tower of the Sussex Street Council School, of 1874, is in the distance to the left. Nearly all the original streets in the area between Edward Street and Albion Hill were rapidly and cheaply built from the early 1800s onwards, as a quick fix to the expanding town's housing needs (in 1780, the population was 3,800 people, by 1831 it would be 40,500). The small view, taken much further up Sussex Street, virtually opposite St John's School, gives a good idea of what most of these houses looked like.

A glance down a directory entry for Sussex Street in the mid-1920s shows what an assortment of buildings, shops and trades could be found there, typical of most streets in this area – a boot maker, grocer, greengrocer, baker, tailor, butcher, a draper, coal and corn merchants, a plating works, an upholsterer, several general stores, a mission hall and any number of pubs and beer shops – all in the one street with houses in between. Despite this bohemian quaintness, it would be the sheer concentration of people and businesses in this area that brought about its demise.

The 1921 Census showed the town's population to be 142,427 which doesn't seem huge now. Then, however, the density of people living in Brighton was second only to London's West Ham. A 1930 Parliamentary slum clearance act gave corporations powers to start clearing slums – which they duly did. In Brighton, it was with particular vigour and speed.

The modern view shows the result of this clearance and subsequent redevelopment. However, although clinics and modern flats were built on the northern side of the street and a market occupies the southern side, something's been lost along the way. The view looks lifeless and sterile and Sussex Street has now lost all its flavour and character; it's now just somewhere to park the car or pass through pretty quickly.

RICHMOND BUILDINGS

Repeat the story of Sussex Street, from the previous pages, with Richmond Buildings, off Richmond Street, seen here, looking north, in 1954. The chimney of the Phoenix Brewery is in the distance. Actually, it's a worse loss, for while Sussex Street still exists, Richmond Buildings doesn't – it was completely obliterated by redevelopment in the 1960s.

This is seen in the 2003 view, where the shops of Richmond Parade stand partly on the site of Richmond Buildings and are typically soulless of their period. At least they are more human in scale than the high-

rise towers that went up nearby to replace the houses of the area.

CLAREMONT ROW

Another view of 'backstreet Brighton', Claremont Row, seen from Richmond Street, looking through to Sussex Street. There were thirty-four houses on the eastern side of the street, but none on the western side, where school buildings each end and their respective playgrounds took up the whole site. The four pictures here show the gradual demise of Claremont Row. The main view shows the street intact in 1935 with Richmond Street School on the right. This was built in 1872 and appears again in the first small picture, of 1960, where the houses on the eastern side have been cleared (as slum clearance) and prefab homes built, during the closing years of World War II, to rehouse families who had lost their homes during bombing.

Claremont Street is the background on the left.

Prefabs were a huge improvement on some of the old houses; they had inside

lavatories, bathrooms and their kitchens were fitted with refrigerators.

The other small view is just a year or so later, when the prefabs had been removed and so had the school (in 1962). The Milner and Kingswood flats (built in 1934 and 1938) can be seen in the distance.

The 2003 view shows everything gone, with Ashton Rise flats covering the site.

93

CARLTON HILL

Carlton Hill is the street here, photographed in the early 1930s, with Nelson Place off to the left. The next street up, by the lamppost, is Nelson Street. The empty corner shop in the foreground (22 Carlton Hill), with its fancy turret window, used to be a butcher's shop, owned by Jonathan Burberry (a town councillor) who started as a butcher in 1878 and whose premises were described in a Brighton guide of 1911 as 'commodious and scrupulously clean ...fulfilling the most acceptable ideals of a first-class meat business'. The smaller photograph shows his shop at this time. However, like everywhere else in the area, it would succumb to 1930s clearance and the redeveloped site (if you can call it that) is shown in the early 1960s view, with the

94

Kingswood flats on the left and the rear of St John's Primary School (later rebuilt) in the mid-distance. The modern view shows flats built in 2003 on the school site, on the eastern side of what was Nelson Street, but is now an extension of John Street. Nelson Street was another casualty of the 1930s slum clearance and it has taken some seven decades to, partly, rebuild this side of it.

PATRIOT PLACE

This is one of the rarest pictures in the book, showing Patriot Place, now Tilbury Place, off Carlton Hill, about 1830. The small terrace here is thought to date from about 1815 and the house at the southern end (seen in the modern view) must date from after 1830 as it's not in the picture. The house was originally the residence of a wealthy merchant and landowner, Edwin Tarner. The drawing shows extensive grounds to the north of the original terrace, belonging to a school. The street was renamed after Tarner's wife, whose maiden name was Tilbury, in 1862, which could be when the house was built. This large property, subsequently St John's Lodge, was left to the council in 1933, becoming a hospice

the following year when it was described as a 'home for persons of very limited means and a brief expectation of life'.

The gardens beyond became a recreation ground in Sussex Street in 1934 and were modernised in the 1980s. The wall on the right was damaged in the hurricane of 1987 and subsequently rebuilt.

The 2003 view shows the far end of Tilbury Place occupied by Prior House, opened in 1936 as headquarters for the Brighton Girl's Club. It's named after Peggy Prior, the club's founder and secretary. This had started life in a small hall in 1928 in Nelson Row, further down Carlton Hill, but was demolished during the slum clearance scheme, leading to the building of the premises here. Prior House became an educational establishment in 1970, but is currently a centre for the unemployed.

THE APOSTOLIC CHURCH

The bottom of Carlton Hill is seen in here, probably in the late 1950s, from the end of Circus Street, with the Catholic Apostolic Church standing between the art college in Grand Parade (out of sight on the right) and William Street, glimpsed on the left. It was an 'Irvingite' church, built in 1865 for a movement founded in the 1830s by Edward Irving, a minister of the Church of Scotland. The church closed in 1954 and was used as student accommodation for a while, but came down in 1964 when the old art college building (1876 – small view) in Grand Parade was completely rebuilt and extended, backing on to William Street.

The top view opposite dates from late 1961, when part of the new art college was almost complete and the old church was due to be cleared for the next stage, reconstructing the

main college building in Grand Parade.

The 2003 comparative view shows the whole site between William Street and Grand Parade occupied by the Faculty of Art and Design (now part of the University of Brighton), which had been opened in June 1967 by the President of the Royal Academy. The architect was Percy Billington.

CUMBERLAND PLACE

Another extremely rare drawing, this time of a street that no longer exits – Cumberland Place, which ran between Edward Street (foreground) and Carlton Hill (distance). Today the site is White Street, the next street up from the huge American Express building in Edward Street.

Cumberland Place appears on a map of 1808 and, with neighbouring Chesterfield Street, Thomas Street and Derby Place, quickly became a seedy neighbourhood and the location for Brighton's Victorian red-light area. The corporation demolished them as slums in 1896 and replaced them with White Street and Blaker Street. White Street was named after Edward White, chairman of the town's sanitary committee, Blaker Street after Sir John Blaker, the Mayor of Brighton from 1895 to 1897.

Old almshouses at the top of Cumberland Place, seen in the small view, survived the redevelopment but came down in 1983-84 so a car park could be laid out in neighbouring Mighell Street. These almshouses were used as Dell's Furniture Repository for a number of years, and in the 1970s housed building materials when the American Express complex was under construction.

White Street received a direct hit from a German bomber during Word War II, in September 1940, resulting in thirteen deaths. The houses blitzed – numbers 6, 8, 10 and 12 – were rebuilt after the war, in a style completely different from those next to them.

The trees on the left in the modern 2003 photograph were planted on the eastern forecourt of American Express in 1979.

PARK PLACE
Still in the Edward Street area, this view of 1934 looks up narrow Park Place towards Carlton Hill, a street of poor housing that would be demolished in the same wave of slum clearance that affected the Sussex Street and Richmond Street

neighbourhood. Also demolished was Mount Pleasant adjoining it to the west (left in the photograph, the backs of the houses can just be seen) and a wider Mount Pleasant was laid out in 1936 (2003 view) built over Park Place, obliterating it completely. The small view shows Edward Street just before all this demolition took place, with the tiny entrance to Park Place left of the lamppost, just past the Vulcan pub, where there's a gap in the line of property. This demonstrates well just how narrow some of these slum streets

were. The wider street on the other side of the pub is the old, original Mount Pleasant.

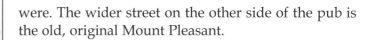

103

HIGH STREET

Off the southern side of Edward Street runs High Street, which never seems important enough to justify its grand name. It was built up during the early 1800s; the view here (1954) of the eastern side shows some of its original houses. The central shop, at 63, 64 and 65, was a yeast merchant's (presumably to supply the many bakeries throughout Brighton at this time). A 1956 directory reveals all manner of establishments in the street prior to most being cleared for the awful St James's House development, built 1965-66. These included a fish and chip shop, hairdresser, car dealer, a pet shop, watchmaker, a small factory that produced electric motors, a wholesale confectioners as well as the premises of Titcombs, the builders, plus some thirty private houses. All long gone now -- 2003 view.

CHAPEL STREET

Chapel Street, running between St James's Street and Edward Street, took its name from neighbouring St James's Chapel, in St James's Street, which opened in 1813 and was demolished in 1950. Like High Street, Chapel Street is another built up during the very early nineteenth century and this picture is a close-up of two of its original cottages (built about 1808) on the western side, photographed in 1954, just before demolition. As can be seen, these were set back a fair distance from the road and had front gardens. What price would they fetch today, if they'd survived and been modernised?

At one time, Chapel Street contained a large number of houses, workshops and stores, virtually all lost now, many cleared for the St James's House flats, seen on the previous page, which straddles a huge site across Chapel Street and adjoining High Street.

ST JAMES'S STREET

St James's Street in 1926, looking west. George Street is off to the right. Very little has changed here over the years and the street is one of the few shopping thoroughfares that hasn't been widened to improve traffic flow (it's been one way though, west to east, since 1968). The street was first built up during the mid-1780s, when the lower part was called Craven Buildings, the upper part, from Charles Street, Prospect Row. The name St James's Street seems to have been adopted for the whole thoroughfare about 1803, taking its name from St James's Palace, in London. However, despite the grand name and recent 'improvements', mainly to the bottom part of St James's Street, the place seems to have become (2003) one of the tackiest thoroughfares in the city and not a pleasant street to walk through at all, particularly the lower part.

ATLINGWORTH STREET

The old photograph here is of Atlingworth Street in the early 1900s, looking from the seafront northwards; the Rock Brewery, in the distance, was at 61 St James's Street. This operated from about 1809 (when it was described as 'newly erected') and had a large number of owners over the years. Brewing lasted until 1928, then the premises were used as a depot.

The huge chimney probably came down about this time. The brewery was finally demolished in 1978. Many old photographs of Brighton have background advertisements on walls or hoardings advertising 'Rock Ales' and there's probably still a pub or two around in the city that has the old brand name etched on its windows or carved on its exterior walls. Atlingworth Street itself has changed little since the old photograph was taken and was built in the early 1830s as Brighton expanded eastwards, due mainly to the patronage of George IV and his successor, William IV, and to fashionable society visiting the town.

ST GEORGE'S ROAD

Another brewery building, which was demolished in the 1970s, stood in Seymour Street, backing onto St George's Road. This was the Kemp Town Brewery and these premises saw beer produced until April 1964.

This brewery came about through a long series of amalgamations. It was established in 1908 by Abbey and Sons, which previously had brewed as Hallett and Abbey. William Hallett was Mayor of Brighton in 1855. He had founded his own Bristol Brewery in the late 1830s.

Charringtons had taken the brewery over in 1954, then moved it to Newhaven (Avis Way) and the redundant property in Seymour Street was demolished in 1970. The main photograph here dates from January that year. The 2003 picture shows the housing that was built on the northern part of the site.

KEMP TOWN RAILWAY STATION
The station at Kemp Town featured in Volume I of this book (page 83), but here's a different view of it, looking south this time, dating from April, 1968.

The Kemp Town railway opened in August 1869 and carried passengers until 1933. Then it operated as a goods line (mainly coal) until finally closing in 1971. It was built to stop rival companies laying a line from London to Brighton, terminating at Kemp Town.

The small view shows the site of the station and yard being redeveloped as the Freshfield Industrial Estate in 1975. It was some hole that was excavated for the railway site back in the 1860s! Old industrial and builders' premises still lined Eastern Road at this time. On the right, towering over the white cars, are the old Albion Flour Mills, which closed in 1923. The site of the railway today (2003) is partly the industrial estate, partly the car park for the Gala Bingo premises.

113

LEWES ROAD VIADUCT

The Kemp Town railway allows this 'then and now' survey of Brighton and Hove to travel to Lewes Road, where the viaduct that took the line across the road and on to Brighton Station is seen under construction in a view of 1869 (workers can just be made out on top). The trees here had been planted about five years earlier. Through the central archway can be seen the strange, castle-like entrance to the Extra-Mural Cemetery of the 1850s.

Some very old cottages can also be seen through the arch on the right. These were known as California Cottages,

which later became part of Melbourne Street.

Once the railway at Kemp Town closed, the viaduct was demolished in sections, the very last part coming down in 1983. Today, this part of Lewes Road still retains a little of its old character, but leads to the dreadful gyratory system, laid out in the 1980s. Like everywhere else where modern redevelopment has taken place, a lot's been lost along the way.

EXTRA-MURAL CEMETERY

Here's a close-up of the entrance to Brighton's old Extra-Mural Cemetery, off Lewes Road, where the first interment took place in November 1851.

This cemetery was run by a private company and the site chosen came about due to new laws, passed in 1848, stipulating that any new burial grounds must be away from the centre of a town or city area, mainly for health reasons. St Nicholas's churchyard, in Dyke Road, was by now full and because the Extra-Mural's charges were high for parochial burials, another new cemetery was duly initiated off Lewes Road adjoining the Extra-Mural, on some two acres of land donated by the Marquess of Bristol. This was run by the corporation, so everyone was assured of a place –

even paupers – and from 1902 it became the Brighton Borough Cemetery. Cremations, the first in Sussex, took place from 1930. The old Extra-Mural company eventually went into liquidation and Brighton Corporation took over in 1956. About the same time the corporation's own neighbouring cemetery took the name Woodvale. The fancy archway was removed in 1961 so that a mortuary could be built (2003 view). The old Extra-Mural Cemetery still exists of course (wonderfully atmospheric) and is entered by passing the mortuary or from a path off the main drive of Woodvale.

ARTHUR H COX & CO

This was Cox's pill factory, which made medicinal creams and tablets, standing where Upper Lewes Road (left) meets Lewes Road (foreground). It was founded in June 1838 by Arthur H Cox (below) who originally ran his business from a small shop in Ship Street. He was Mayor of Brighton from 1882 to 1883. He moved to Lewes Road early in 1911, occupying what

were old laundry premises; his main claim to fame would be inventing and patenting the sugar-coated pill.

The old Victorian premises were difficult to upgrade in line with modern hygiene requirements and the firm was forced to move in 1979 to a new factory in the Whiddon Valley, Barnstaple, Devon.

The factory came down in 1983, along with the last section of the Lewes Road viaduct, and the site today is occupied by a huge Sainsbury's store. The main façade of this was given arches as a reminder of the lost viaduct and the clock from the old factory was installed up near the roof line. The store opened in April 1985.

LONDON ROAD
Another of the city's main roads is seen in this view of London Road, taken probably in the 1920s. The buildings in the background, although shops in this picture, were obviously all once fine, individual houses and London Road (first

known as Queen's Road) was almost entirely residential when first built up.

Trams, seen in the distance, played a vital role in opening up the area to commercial development and provided a cheap and reliable source of transport to and from London Road for those doing their shopping.

Dominating the street in the old view is the massive church of St Bartholomew, facing Ann Street, opened in 1874. This is easily

Brighton and Hove's most remarkable and spectacular church and one of the most unique buildings of its kind anywhere in the world. It is the tallest church in Britain, being one metre higher than Westminster Abbey. It's always said, but probably untrue (sadly), that St Bartholomew's was built to the measurements given in the Bible for Noah's Ark.

Here is an example of a building hugely out of scale with everything around it. It was derided in its day as 'a cheese warehouse,' 'a monstrous excrescence,' 'uselessly large' and 'painfully ugly and sadly out of place'.

The church brought huge wrath down on the head of its builder, Arthur Douglas Wagner, mentioned on page 74. The architect was the little-known Edmund Scott. Today the church is regarded as a jewel in the city's architectural crown, on a par with the Royal Pavilion, the squares and crescents of the Kemp Town and Brunswick estates and the West Pier (when it was operative). In the 2003 view (above) the church is lost behind the central shop – for many years Marks and Spencer – but the cross is just visible.

BEACONSFIELD VILLAS

On to the outskirts of the city now and a rare view of Beaconsfield Villas taken in April 1901, looking from Stanford Avenue to the top of the hill. Tracks are being laid for the tram system about to be adopted by the town. It was up and running seven months after this view was taken. This part of Beaconsfield Villas was a late Victorian development, dating from the early 1880s. Further up, the houses date from a few

years later.

In the modern view, the buildings are virtually identical, the trams have long since stopped running (withdrawn in 1939) and the trees, hardly visible in the early view, have since put on a sturdy growth.

DITCHLING ROAD

A similar situation in Ditchling Road, again in April 1901, where the tram system is being laid out. Grantham Road is on the left. This lower part of Ditchling Road was built up in the late 1890s, the upper part a few years later. Ditchling Road, at nearly three and a quarter miles in length, is the third longest thoroughfare in Brighton. It leads – eventually – to the village of Ditchling, hence the name. (Lewes Road is longest road in Brighton, Marine Drive the second.)

The track-laying here is one stage on from the work seen on the previous page, as this view shows wooden blocks being positioned, tightly packed around the tracks. When given a coat of tarmac this would form the final road surface.

The modern view is little changed – just far more cars.

DYKE ROAD

Dyke Road now, seen in 1897, with hardly a building or vehicle in sight. The old, roped fence marked the boundary between Brighton and Preston at this time. The road led to Devil's Dyke, a popular beauty spot to the north west of Brighton and Hove (see pages 142-143).

The smaller 1950s view shows redevelopment on both sides of the widened road. On the left is the border of Dyke Road Park, which opened to the public in

September 1924. On the other side the most prominent building is Highcroft, to the right, often referred to as the Drill Hall, built in 1939 on the eve of World War II for the training of newly recruited soldiers. Today it is the Quebec TA Centre, B (Royal Sussex) Company, but is lost in the 2003 view amid the trees and traffic.

CHURCH OF ST NICHOLAS

Where Dyke Road descends to border the north west corner of the Old Town area, and is virtually a continuation of North Street, stands Brighton's most ancient church, St Nicholas. It's seen in a very old photograph here, of about 1850. The church dates from the fourteenth century, but was so over-restored by the Victorians in 1853 (after this view was taken) that only the pillars and arches of the nave, the chancel arch and tower are of any great antiquity. An interesting monument inside is to the Duke of Wellington, who attended the church as a child. Buried in the churchyard are Martha Gunn, the bathing proprietress, architect Amon Wilds, Nicholas Tettersall and Sake Dene Mahomed, who introduced Turkish baths to Britain.

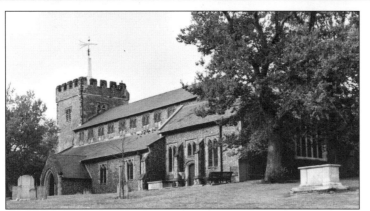

The modern view shows the haphazard graveyard rearranged (this took place after World War II), and one tomb lost in the 'tidying up' was that of 'Smoaker Miles', the male equivalent of Martha Gunn, who oversaw the bathing of the Prince of Wales, later George IV, when taking a dip off Brighton beach. After the great storm of 1987, some ninety trees were lost, again changing the appearance of the place.

THE DIALS CONGREGATIONAL CHURCH

Another church off Dyke Road, but one that no longer exists. This was the Dials Congregational Church at the corner of Clifton Road, seen here not long before demolition in the spring of 1972. Designed by local architect Thomas Simpson, with a horseshoe-shaped interior, this was built in 1870-71 and had an extremely tall tower, 150ft high, giving the building a distinctive, continental appearance. It looked like something one might encounter sailing down the Rhine. In 1969 it was sold for £30,000 for redevelopment, and demolished in the spring of 1972. Sheltered accommodation, built in 1985-86, now mostly occupies the site.

WESTERN ROAD

To Western Road now, looking east from the corner of Clarence Square (right) in 1902. The flags are out to celebrate the coronation of Edward VII, which took place in August that year (postponed from July, because he had developed acute appendicitis). The building on the corner, where an umbrella has been painted, was rebuilt in 1908. All the buildings on the left would be demolished in stages for the widening of Western Road. A small part was widened in 1912, but it wasn't until the 1920s that work started in earnest and carried on for another decade. The widening accounts for the lack of buildings on the left of the 2003 view as they are set well back from the line of the old ones.

THE BRIGHTON AND HOVE BORDER

More royal connections with this photograph taken in Western Road on the exact border between Brighton and Hove. It's July 1881 and a commemorative arch straddles the road, prepared for the visit of Edward, Prince of Wales (crowned Edward VII in 1902), his wife, Princess Alexandra, and their children. Would the council or any group in the city go to all this trouble for a royal visit today? This castle-like structure was

only a temporary affair, like a stage set, and came down after the visit. The royal couple (left) performed several civic functions during their visit to Brighton, the main one being the opening of the Royal Alexandra Children's Hospital in Dyke Road, which was named in honour of the princess.

DENMARK VILLAS AND THE GOLD STONE

Strange to see sheep grazing in Denmark Villas. This view, unfortunately somewhat faded, dates from about 1870. The road of Eaton Villas would eventually cut across the foreground. Hove was a slow developer compared with Brighton during the Victorian period, and many people owned houses with farmland literally on their doorsteps.

This part of Denmark Villas probably dates from the

1850s and the picture shows its western side directly adjoining a field of Longbarn Farm, sometimes known as Rigden's Farm, after the farmer who ran it, well-known for his connection with Hove's Goldstone, the huge rock on display in Hove Park. The smaller view of September 1900 shows the stone being dug up on Rigden's land, after he'd had it buried in the 1830s (possibly a bit later) to put an end to tiresome archaeologists traipsing over his crops to examine it. Since 1906 it's been displayed in the park. All sorts of ideas have been put forward about the stone's origins, a Druid's altar from some ancient site in the area being one of the more fanciful.

ST ANN'S WELL GARDENS

Several buildings in St Ann's Well Gardens no longer exist. Its most famous, the Well House, is seen here in the 1920s before demolition was approved in 1937. For years this was simply known as the chalybeate at Brighton and operated long before the park surrounded it and the garden name was adopted (by the Victorians). Its spring waters were supposed to be very beneficial for all sorts of ills and disorders and Dr Richard Russell (pages 30-31) wholeheartedly recommended the

waters and paid to have a proper basin built around it. George IV's illegal wife, Maria Fitzherbert, came and drank the waters here. In the late Victorian period, the spring was producing an amazing 300 gallons a day, but the sinking of an artesian well in the area in the early twentieth century caused the spring to all but dry up. This and the general decline in popularity of taking the waters led to the building's eventual demolition. The twelve acres of St Ann's Well Gardens became a public park in May 1908.

WEST WAY – DYKE RAILWAY EMBANKMENT

An astonishing 'here and now' comparison, with the 'old' view showing a huge chalk mound being removed behind what would become the site of Hangleton library in West Way (2003 view).

A railway to the Devil's Dyke operated from September 1887 until December 1938. The route was via the Shoreham line, branching off at Aldrington, then winding north west across countryside where eventually roads like Amherst Crescent, Rowan Avenue and Poplar Avenue would subsequently be built. It was a very slow journey, due to the trains having to travel continuously uphill. For some reason the station at the Dyke was situated half a mile from the hotel area and 200 yards below it (small view), which meant quite a walk to the summit once visitors had arrived at the station. The increasing use of cars to reach the Dyke affected trade and brought about the demise of the railway. Dismantling the line wasn't just a case of taking up the rails, it meant all sorts of filling in either side of embankments or, as in the old view here, levelling one out ready for the site to be redeveloped with housing and new roads.

WEST BLATCHINGTON WINDMILL

To West Blatchington now and the famous windmill is seen in 1938 before the tide of urban redevelopment swallowed up this then picturesque rural area. The six-sided smock mill was built about 1820 and it's known that John Constable sketched it in November 1825. It was part of what for many years was Court Farm – 700 acres – and ceased working in 1897 when two of the sweeps blew off in a storm. On the left is St Peter's Church, built 1890-91 and enlarged in 1960.

West Blatchington mill was built on a square base from which three barns radiated. One was lost in a fire in May,

1936 and now only one remains. Hove Corporation acquired the mill in 1939 plus five acres of land, the farm having been given up. The corporation undertook basic restoration of the mill and laid out Holmes Avenue either side of it – named after farmer Holmes, who ran the neighbouring Gibbets Farm (so-called as an old hanging post used to stand on its land, just north of Old Shoreham Road).

It wasn't until the 1970s that work on the full restoration of West Blatchington Windmill started; it opened to the public in July 1980. A visitor's centre and lecture hall have recently opened under the mill.

The 2003 photograph shows the site covered by Hangleton Road and its houses, with the old windmill just visible in the distance, left of the lamp post.

HANGLETON LANE

Hangleton Lane, looking west, in 1930; the land here was part of Broomfield Farm, where Alfred Cross was the tenant farmer for many years. In the 2003 view a tarmac road, housing and plenty of cars have long since replaced the muddy track and horse and cart of the old picture. A feed road from Old Shoreham Road to the Brighton Bypass now stands a short distance from where the view was taken and a huge Sainsbury's store operates just down the road.

A surprising number of outlying farms were given up in the Brighton and Hove area (and the rest of the country) during the 1930s. This was due to a variety of circumstances, the decline starting in World War I, when

the army requisitioned many farm horses for troop and transport use. Along with the slump following the war, more intensive farming methods being introduced and owners being offered large sums of money for land by property developers (exactly what happened in Hangleton and West Blatchington), many farms were sold off. Today, one or two are left (Stanmer and Mile Oak) but most lay buried and forgotten under housing estates and modern roads.

DEVIL'S DYKE

The final scene is well out of Brighton and Hove; here's the carriage park outside the hostelry at Devil's Dyke. It's seen about 1906, with carriages bringing visitors from Brighton to the Dyke for a day out. A close-up of one of these 'brakes', as they were sometimes called, is seen in the smaller view. The return fare in 1899 was 1s 6d (about 8p today). The railway station would be well down the road off to the left. Apart from the pub and restaurant, and the inevitable

cars in the 2003 picture, the grounds have changed little over the intervening 100 years. The startling view north-westwards from the hill hasn't changed much either and it's easy to stand looking across the weald, with time seeming to slip away as you realise you are seeing virtually the same vista our Victorian forefathers did – which can't of course be said for the majority of views in this second 'then and now' survey of Brighton and Hove, which ends here.

Photo: Ray Ede

ABOUT THE AUTHOR

Chris Horlock was born in White Street, Brighton, in September 1953 and went to Park Street Infants School (demolished in 1986), St Luke's Terrace Junior School (still there) and the Secondary Technical School, Hanover Terrace (demolished in 2000), where his best subjects were art, English and history. He undertook four years of teacher-training at what was then Brighton College of Education, Falmer, and his first teaching post was from 1976 at Glebe Middle School, Southwick. He is at present Subject Co-Ordinator of History and Geography at Thomas A Becket Middle School, Worthing, the second largest middle school in the country. He's been married fourteen years to Roz and has two children, Charlotte and George, aged eleven and seven respectively.

Chris's books on Brighton have been immensely successful over the last four years and he's received letters from all over the world from people who have somehow obtained copies of them – one has even been spotted in a toilet in a German pub! And there's no let up. Future plans include *Bizarre Brighton,* a book detailing all the weird and wonderful stories, facts and figures about the city Chris has discovered or been told over the years, plus *Brighton : The Sixties,* another photographic survey, this time concentrating solely on the decade 1960-70. His play *Magpie's Child* received great acclaim in the 2003 Brighton Festival and he has another theatrical piece in the pipeline, *Dubious Charms,* which will be staged as soon as he can finish it! Chris also writes a monthly column in *Brighton and Hove Life* and continues to travel all over Sussex giving talks on aspects of Brighton and Hove's history.